Getting To Know...

Nature's Children

CHIMPANZEES

Caroline Greenland

SCHOLASTIC INC.

New York   Toronto   London   Auckland   Sydney
Mexico City   New Delhi   Hong Kong   Buenos Aires

Facts in Brief

Classification of Common Chimpanzees
Class: *Mammalia* (mammals)
Order: *Primates* (monkeys, apes, people)
Family: *Pongidae* (people-like apes)
Genus: *Pan*
Species: *Pan troglodytes*

World distribution.   West and central Africa.

Habitat.   Rain forest, woodland and grassland.

Distinctive physical characteristics.   Common Chimpanzees have arms that are longer than legs and opposable thumbs and big toes.

Habits.   Live in communities, ranging from 15 to 80 chimpanzees, and are active during the day.

Diet.   Mainly fruit; but also leaves, seeds, bark, buds, blossoms, bird eggs, insects, honey, and occasionally birds and other mammals.

Published by Scholastic Inc.
90 Old Sherman Turnpike, Danbury, Connecticut 06816.

ISBN: 0-7172-6716-4   Printed in the U.S.A.

Have you ever wondered . . .

In the thickest part of the African jungle, a loud hoot is heard. Birds fly away in fright. Excited screams are followed by more hooting and shrieking. Suddenly the trees are filled with chimpanzees swinging through the branches toward the noise. One chimp has found a tree filled with ripe fruit, and it has called to all its friends. Soon they are feasting on the delicious fruit and chattering to each other.

As you can tell from this, chimpanzees are very *sociable*—and they're also very intelligent. Turn the page to learn more about these fascinating animals.

A Chimp Family

A mother chimp gently cradles her month-old baby in her arms. Her older youngster, now five years old, is fascinated with this new member of the family. As he reaches out to touch the furry little bundle, his mother pushes his hand away and turns her back on him.

It is hard for the youngster now that he is no longer the center of his mother's attention. She used to like to play with him. He shouldn't worry though. In a few months, his baby sister will be stronger and bigger. Then he will be able to teach her how to play tag and dangle from a tree with only one hand—and how to grab their mother's ear when she's looking the other way.

Even high up in a treetop, this baby chimp seems to feel perfectly safe and content in its mother's arms.

Big Apes, Little Apes

Chimpanzees belong to a group of animals called *Primates*, which includes apes and monkeys. The larger apes are known as great apes. These include gorillas, orangutans, and chimpanzees. The lesser apes, which are smaller, are gibbons and siamangs. Apes differ from monkeys in several ways. Apes do not have tails, and they are bigger than monkeys. Compared to monkeys, apes also have larger brains and are considered to be more intelligent.

Many scientists believe that apes and human beings had a common ancestor long, long ago. Certainly apes have many similarities with people. They can stand upright; they have large brains; and their bodies, muscles, and blood types are similar to ours. And apes often behave exactly the same way we do.

In the wild, chimpanzees may live to be almost 40 years old.

Opposite page:

*Pygmy Chimp.
The reason both
the Common and
Pygmy chimps
stay on their own
sides of the Zaire
River is simple:
chimpanzees
cannot swim.*

Land of the Chimpanzees

There are two kinds of chimps, the Common Chimpanzee and the Pygmy, or *Bonobo,* Chimpanzee. The difference between them is not that one is much smaller than the other, as you might expect. Instead, the Pygmy Chimpanzee has longer legs, a lighter build, and a more rounded head. It also has a black face, whereas the Common Chimpanzee's face is usually light.

The Pygmy Chimpanzee is found in *rain forests* in central Africa, between the Zaire and Kasai rivers. The Common Chimpanzee is found north of the Zaire River in west and central Africa.

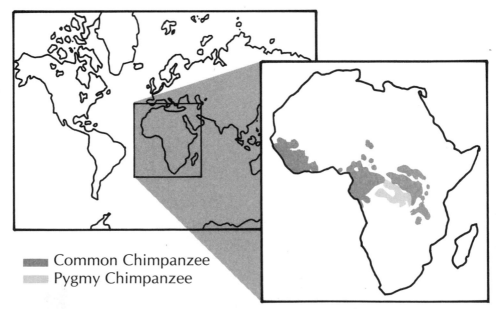

◼ Common Chimpanzee
◼ Pygmy Chimpanzee

Male chimps may perform displays to show others how strong they are.

Rain, Rain, Go Away

The area where chimpanzees live in Africa is near the equator. Temperatures there can vary from a very hot day (108°F or 42°C) to a cool night (50°F or 10°C). Throughout much of the chimpanzee's habitat there is a rainy season. From December to March, it rains for long periods of time.

During rainstorms male chimps sometimes perform noisy *displays,* screaming and throwing things. Youngsters swing wildly through the trees as if they are trying to dodge the raindrops. Females may make nests and try to sleep through the storms. The only chimps that stay dry are the babies, snugly nestled between their mother's chest and arms.

Luckily, chimpanzees' thick coats help keep them warm even when they get wet. Once they are soaked, they often just sit in the open looking miserable. Intelligent as they are, they do not build shelters. However, when the rain finally stops, they dry themselves off with leaves.

Hand

Foot

Weighing In

Chimpanzees are about the same size as a ten-year-old child. Most are about 3 feet (1 meter) tall with a few growing to 5 1/2 feet (1.7 meters). Adult males usually weigh 99 to 176 pounds (45 to 80 kilograms), though a large one may tip the scales at 198 pounds (90 kilograms). The females are shorter and lighter.

Although they look quite similar to humans, chimps' arms are longer than their legs. They also have very long fingers and *opposable thumbs,* just like you. This means that chimps can move their thumb around to meet their fingers, which allows them to pick up things easily. Chimps also have opposable big toes, so they can climb trees and grasp branches with their feet much more easily than you can.

The Common Chimpanzee can be found in rain forests, woodlands, and grasslands dotted with trees.

Swinging Through the Trees

Although chimpanzees can walk upright, they only do so if they are angry, if their hands are full, or if they are trying to see over tall grass. When chimps are on the ground, they usually *"knuckle walk,"* which means they walk on all fours by supporting the front part of their body on their knuckles, not their palms.

Chimpanzees spend more than one-third of their time in trees. Their extra-long palms and fingers give them a special hook-grip that allows them to swing easily from branch to branch. Their opposable thumbs and big toes help to make them fast and steady climbers.

"Now what do I do?"

Sensible Senses

Do you think you would be able to sneak up on a chimp? No way! Chimps have large ears that stick out from the sides of their head. They can catch even the smallest sounds. They also have a keen sense of smell, which helps them to find food and sniff out intruders. Their eyes face forward, and they have the ability to perceive depth and color. This allows them to spot ripe fruit amidst the thick vegetation, where they live. And with their excellent eyesight, they notice everything that is going on around them.

Both male and female chimps may become bald as they grow older. You can tell this is a male chimp because of his triangular-shaped bald patch.

Chimp Communities

Chimpanzees live in *communities* of 15 to 80 members. Although they roam through a *territory* of up to 24 square miles (60 square kilometers), they spend most of their time each day in a small area of under 1.5 square miles (4 square kilometers). The whole community is rarely seen together. Instead, smaller groups form for one or two days and then separate. New groups are constantly being formed. The only chimps that see each other daily are the family groups made up of a mother and her young offspring. Males may form temporary groups for patrolling the borders of their territory and for socializing.

Although different chimpanzee communities may have overlapping ranges, it is difficult to know how they will react when they meet. Sometimes strangers are ignored and sometimes they are accepted. At other times, they are attacked and driven away by groups of males.

Chimps do not swim, but they will go into shallow water to cool off.

Opposite page:

*How do you think
this chimpanzee is
feeling?*

Getting the Point Across

If you were pretending to be a chimp, how
would you act? Most people would pant and
hoot while jumping up and down. When a
chimp behaves like this, it is excited or happy
about something.

Chimpanzees seem to have many of the
same emotions as humans—chimps can feel
happy, sad, angry, or frightened. They show
their feelings in different ways, just as we do.
Chimps use sounds such as hoots, grunts, and
whimpers. Their faces can show all kinds of
expressions, including smiles and pouts. Body
language is another way of letting others know
how they feel. There is no mistaking a happy
young chimp. It uses its whole body by
twirling and somersaulting.

Chimpanzees are sociable animals. They
greet old friends with hugs and kisses. They
also like to hold hands and pat each other on
the back. A frightened chimp may reach out to
touch a member of its community to reassure
itself. And if a chimp feels threatened, it
stands upright and bristles its hair to make
itself look bigger.

Loud, Louder, Loudest

Imagine a fierce thunderstorm passing over an African forest. Rain is pelting down and lightning is flashing across the sky. The tree branches sway with the wind. Suddenly a male chimpanzee charges down a hill, swinging his arms wildly and screaming. He rips a branch from the nearest tree and beats the ground as he bounds through the wet grass. Then up a tree he leaps, only to come crashing down with more loud hoots. Is he crazy? No, he is behaving the way many male chimps do in a thunderstorm. He is performing what is called a display.

Why a male chimp may display when there is a storm is something of a mystery, but on other occasions, the reason for this noisy performance is more obvious. He is showing other males how strong he is.

You will hardly ever see a chimp relaxing in the sun—it prefers the shade.

What's for Lunch?

More than half of a chimp's waking hours are spent eating, and much of the rest of its time is spent looking for food. Most of what a chimp likes to eat grows on trees. Fruit, leaves, seeds, and bark all taste good to a chimp.

Fruit is one of the chimpanzee's favorite things to eat. Within their territory, chimps know the exact location of all the different fruit trees. They even remember from one season to the next when the fruit will ripen.

When ripe figs are found, a chimp is not selfish. It barks, pants, and hoots to announce the good news to other chimps in the community. Soon it will be joined by more chimps that grin and pat each other on the back before settling down to eat.

As well as vegetation, chimps also eat bird eggs, insects, and honey. Once in a while, they eat birds, antelopes, bush pigs, and even monkeys, although they have no organized system for hunting.

Tasty twigs.

Fishing for Termites

Chimpanzees are considered to be one of the most intelligent animals. They are able to solve problems by using their brains. And like people, they have developed the ability to use tools.

Now, a chimp likes a tasty meal of termites, but it isn't easy to get at termites when they are inside their rock-hard mound. So a chimp finds a small twig or a thick blade of grass and trims it until it's just the right size to use as a "fishing rod." Then the chimp pokes the rod into a hole in the mound. The termites bite it, and the chimp pulls it out and removes the insects with its lips. Delicious!

A young Pygmy Chimpanzee plucks insects off blades of grass for a quick snack.

Tool Box

Chimps also use tools for many other reasons besides catching termites. They use sticks and rocks to break the hard outer coverings of some types of fruit. And when there isn't much water around, chimpanzees will make "sponges" to soak up water. First they chew up a mouthful of leaves. Then they roll the leaves into a ball and place it in a damp hole in a tree or wherever else hard-to-reach water is found. Finally they squeeze the sponge to have a cool drink.

In addition, chimps sometimes use rocks and branches as weapons against other animals.

A cool drink on a hot day is quite refreshing.

Looking Good

You use a comb or brush to keep your hair tidy. Chimps use their fingers and lips to *groom* themselves and each other. Two chimps sit close together. One chimp parts the other's hair and looks for old bits of skin and salt, which it then removes with nimble fingers or lips. It may surprise you to know that chimps do not have fleas. They do have the occasional tick or louse, however, which then become crunchy, tasty treats!

Keeping neat and clean is not the main reason for grooming. More often than not, a chimp is groomed when it is excited or worried. Grooming feels good and it helps calm down an upset chimp. Also, grooming helps the members of a community to feel close to one another. This sociable activity may go on for hours and may include as many as ten chimpanzees.

Adult chimps usually spend an hour or so a day grooming.

This chimp has found a cool, comfortable spot to rest.

Night Nests

How would you like to make your bed every day—from scratch? Chimps do. In fact, sometimes they even make two beds a day. One is for sleeping in at night, and the other is for their afternoon nap.

How do they do it? First they select a strong base. A fork in a tree or two branches close together will do. This may be 33 feet (10 meters) above the ground—about as high up as the top of a telephone pole. Next the chimp forms a mattress by bending branches to cover the base. Each branch is held in place by one of the chimp's feet until the next branch is bent. Small twigs and leaves are then stuffed into the mattress to make it soft. Now for the test: the chimp lies down to see if its bed is comfortable. If the bed is not to its liking, more leaves are plucked and placed in the hard spots.

The only time a bed is shared is when a mother has a youngster under four years old. Young chimps are capable of making their own beds long before this, but they seem to enjoy the companionship of their mother at night.

Mating

Chimpanzees can *mate* at any time of the year. Females are able to give birth after the age of six. At mating time, females are given special treatment in their community. They are groomed more often and food is shared with them. The females can relax and enjoy this unusual situation.

A female may sometimes mate with many males in her community. At other times, the strongest male will chase away all the other males. Then he and the female go off alone together for days or even weeks. The baby is born eight months later. Chimps rarely give birth to twins.

A mother chimp is fiercely protective of her baby.

Bouncing Baby

A baby chimp is smaller than a human baby. It usually weighs less than 4.4 pounds (2 kilograms) and has a white tuft on its rump, which fades as it grows older.

At first the little chimp is almost as helpless as a human baby. It cannot hold its head up or grasp its mother's hair. The mother chimp uses one arm to cradle her youngster close to her breast. This means she only has one free arm to use as she moves along the ground or through the trees. She must also stop often to *nurse* her little one. Its mother's milk will be its most important food for the next three or four years.

The other chimps in the community are curious and crowd around to take a peek. But not until the baby is a few months old will the mother allow them to touch her little one.

It isn't long before a baby chimp begins to take an interest in its surroundings.

Playful Chimps

At about six months old, it is time for the youngster to start riding piggyback. Its mother gives it a boost onto her back and starts to walk slowly. At first the little one slips under her tummy in the old familiar riding position. But it must learn, so she pushes it back on top. After many tries and several weeks, the youngster can hold on no matter how fast the mother moves.

Baby chimps spend a lot of time playing as they grow older. They love being tickled by their mother. They also enjoy pulling on her ears and wrestling. All of these activities help the youngster to become more coordinated and agile.

After a hard day of playing, it's nice to have a piggyback ride.

Growing Up

Soon the young chimp wants to explore the world beyond its mother's back. This means walking—on twos and fours!

You know how hard it is for human babies to figure out how to crawl. Well, the same is true for chimps. They get their hands and feet all mixed up and spend a lot of time falling on their faces. But by their first birthday, chimps will be able to scamper along after the other youngsters in the community.

Now it's time for them to tackle trees. Wow—this is easy! After all, a chimp can dangle from a branch using one foot. You could do that, too, if your feet looked like your hands.

"Don't worry, I won't let you fall."

Lessons to Learn

A young chimpanzee learns by watching its mother. After it is one year old, it helps her to build a nest to sleep in. The youngster also watches her fish for termites and tries to do the same. After many attempts, the young chimp is able to get a few termites. The youngster's skills will improve quickly.

Young chimps do not leave their mothers until they are five to seven years old. It takes that long for them to learn everything they need to know. The females usually go on to new communities while the males stay in the community where they were born. And in a few years, they are ready to have families of their own.

Words To Know

Bonobo   Another name for the Pygmy Chimpanzee.

Community   A group of the same kind of animals living together.

Display   A noisy performance made by a male chimpanzee during a thunderstorm or to impress other males.

Groom   To clean or brush, especially hair.

Knuckle walk   When an animal, such as a chimpanzee or gorilla, walks on all fours but supports the front part of its body on its knuckles.

Mate   To come together to produce young. Either member of an animal pair is also the other's mate.

Nurse   To drink milk from a mother's body.

Opposable thumb   The kind of thumb that is separated from the fingers and can be moved around to meet them. Humans and a few animals, including chimpanzees, have opposable thumbs.

Primate   An animal that belongs to the order Primates, such as a chimpanzee, monkey, or human being.

Rain forest   Lush tropical forest with heavy rainfall.

Sociable   The term used to describe animals that like the companionship of others of the same species.

Territory   An area that an animal, or a group of animals, lives in and often defends from other animals of the same kind.

Index

PHOTO CREDITS
Cover: George Holton (Photo Researchers). **Interiors:** Photo Researchers, 4, 7, 24; Walter Chandoha, 8; Nancy Adams, 11, 27, 28, 39; Gerard Fritz (Canapress/Uniphoto Picture Agency), 12; Stella Brewer (WWF-Photolibrary), 15, 16; Bill Ivy, 19; Jay Foreman (Unicorn Stock Photos), 20; Cincinnati Zoo, 23; Stephen Krasemann (Peter Arnold/Hot Shots), 31; Tom McHugh (Photo Researchers), 32, 43, 44; Philippe Oberle (WWF-Photolibrary), 35; George Holton (Photo Researchers), 36-7, 40.

Getting To Know...

Nature's Children

LIZARDS

Bill Ivy

SCHOLASTIC INC.

New York   Toronto   London   Auckland   Sydney
Mexico City   New Delhi   Hong Kong   Buenos Aires

Facts in Brief

Classification of lizards
    Class: *Reptilia* (reptiles)
    Order: *Squamata* (lizards and snakes)
    Suborder: *Sauria=Lacertilla* (lizards, geckos, and iguanas)

World distribution. Depends on species. More than 3,000 species of lizards are found on all continents except Antarctica.

North American distribution. Found as far north as southern Canada.

Distinctive physical characteristics. Many lizards have the ability to shed part or all of their tail in order to escape predators. Smaller lizards can regrow their tail in a month; larger ones may take a year to regrow.

Habitat, Habits, Diet. Varies with species.

Size. Varies with species, ranging from 3/4 inch (20 millimeters) in length to more than 10 feet (3 meters).

Published by Scholastic Inc.
90 Old Sherman Turnpike, Danbury, Connecticut 06816.

ISBN: 0-7172-6716-4   Printed in the U.S.A.

Have you ever wondered . . .

If you have ever been lucky enough to see a lizard in the wild, you probably just got a glimpse of it as it scurried by. Lizards are both shy and extremely quick, and most people know very little about them. This is unfortunate because lizards are among the most amazing animals in the world. They come in all sizes, shapes, and colors. Some are tiny, legless, wormlike creatures, while others are the size of a large dog.

There are lizards that can sail through the air, deep-sea dive, change color, walk on ceilings, or eat pigs. To find out more surprising things about lizards, read on.

Land of the Lizard

Lizards are found in all parts of the world except in polar regions. In fact, there is at least one species of lizard on every continent except Antarctica. More than 3,000 *species* have been identified so far.

The majority of lizards live in tropical and subtropical climates, where it is warm all year round. Some can also be found, however, in areas where winters are cold. There, they must *hibernate* underground during the winter months to survive.

Wherever they live, these incredible creatures make themselves at home in a wide variety of environments, from tropical rain forests to deserts and from mountains to lowland plains.

In North America, lizards live as far north as southern Canada.

This Anole Iguana blends in well with its chosen resting spot.

Lizard Relatives

Lizards are *reptiles*, as are snakes, crocodiles, alligators, and turtles. Like all reptiles, lizards are *cold-blooded*, which means they cannot generate their own body heat. But lizards are not usually cold—they get warmth from their surroundings. Lizards lie in the sun to warm up and rest in the shade to cool down. Some types can change color to regulate their temperature— they turn darker to absorb more heat or lighter to absorb less.

Lizards are often mistaken for *salamanders*, but there are several ways to tell them apart. Salamanders, like frogs, are *amphibians*. They have smooth, moist skin, while lizards are covered with *scales*. Salamanders have four fingers on their front limbs, but lizards have five. Also, while lizards love being in the sun, salamanders avoid it.

Although some lizards are legless and look like snakes, there are a few ways to tell who's who. Snakes do not have moveable eyelids, but most lizards do and most lizards have ear openings whereas snakes do not.

Opposite page:
The Red-spotted Newt (bottom), like most salamanders, spends part of its life underwater, breathing through gills. Lizards never have gills. Few of them spend any time at all in water, and those that do have to come up regularly for air. (Top: Common Iguana)

Scaly Skin

Have you ever held a lizard? If not, what do you think it feels like? You might think it would feel wet and slimy, but that's not the case. Actually, lizards are covered from head to tail with scales and are dry to the touch.

Scales are made of *keratin*—the same thing your fingernails are made of. The scales of some lizards are smooth and shiny, while those of other types are as rough as a pinecone. No matter what they look like, scales give the lizard a thick waterproof coat. And they help keep moisture in so that the lizard doesn't dry out in the sun.

What do you think happens as a lizard grows bigger and its scaly skin becomes too small? It sheds the outer layer for a new, larger coat that has been forming underneath.

The chameleon, like most lizards, sheds its skin in patches rather than all at once the way snakes do.

Sense Abilities

Most lizards have excellent vision, and by looking at their eyes you can often learn a lot about their habits. Lizards with round pupils are commonly active during the day, while those with vertical slits are usually creatures of the night. Burrowing lizards have transparent eyelids that protect their eyes from sand and dirt.

Lizards also have a sharp sense of smell. Like you, they smell with their nose, but some also pick up scents in another way—by sticking out their tongue! When a lizard flicks out its tongue, it picks up tiny scent particles from the air. In the lizard's mouth, two special organs called *Jacobson's organs* allow the lizard to taste the air. Lizards may use their tongue to smell nearby food or to sense what kind of environment they're in. But only one type, the chameleon, uses its tongue to actually catch its food.

Lizards have ears but they don't have earflaps as you do. Their ear openings are on the same level as their skin or just below it. Burrowing lizards have small ear openings or none at all.

Opposite page:
If you look closely, you can see the ear opening on this Emerald Swift's head at the edge of its mouth.

Opposite page:

If you're a hungry iguana, nothing hits the spot like a crunchy katydid.

On the Menu

How would you like these for dinner—ants, centipedes, spiders, worms, and slugs? Not very appetizing, you say? To a lizard this would be a feast!

Many lizards feed almost entirely on insects and other small *invertebrates*. Some prefer a diet of plants or fruit, however. Marine Iguanas, for instance, eat only algae. The larger lizards also eat animals, such as clams, mice, and even other lizards. One species, the Komodo Dragon, eats dead animals and occasionally catches a small wild pig or a domestic sheep!

Lizards do not have very good table manners and often just swallow their food whole. Large *prey* is pulled apart and eaten a mouthful at a time.

Most lizards get the water they need by lapping up raindrops and dew. But some desert species rarely get a chance to drink. Fortunately, the plants they eat usually provide enough water for their needs.

Happy Birthday

During the *mating season,* a male lizard chases a female and they *mate.* The couple may stay together for one or more seasons.

Lizards, like birds, produce eggs. The eggs are usually oval shaped with shells that are soft and leathery. A female may lay from 1 to 25 eggs, depositing them most often in a warm, humid place, such as underneath leaf litter and logs.

A few species of lizards guard their eggs, but most lizards just leave them to hatch on their own. When the baby lizard is ready, it uses the razor-sharp egg tooth on its snout to break free of its shell. The egg tooth falls off within a few days. Newborn lizards, most of which look a lot like their parents, are able to take care of themselves as soon as they hatch. They will mature three months to two years later.

Some species of lizards, especially those in cold climates, keep the eggs in their body until they hatch, then they give birth to live young. They do this so that the eggs stay warm.

Opposite page:

A Common Iguana emerges from its shell looking like a small version of its parents. On the other hand, young Jackson's Chameleons (overleaf) obviously change a good deal as they mature.

When faced with an enemy, Australia's Frilled Lizard extends its frill and opens its mouth wide to make itself look as big and as scary as possible.

Self-Defense

If you were a lizard, you would not want to meet a raccoon, otter, fox, opossum, snake, hawk, or badger. Any one of these animals would enjoy having you for lunch. So might a few lizards that are bigger than you.

Fortunately, lizards have a few tricks to help them survive these dangers. When it senses an enemy, a lizard may freeze. Because its color often blends in with its surroundings, it can be very hard to see when it is not moving. If this doesn't work, the lizard may run, hide, hiss, play dead, or even squirt blood from its eyelids!

Each species has its own way of protecting itself. But the most amazing defense of all is common to many species—a detachable tail! When grabbed from behind, the lizard's tail breaks off cleanly and wiggles around on the ground by itself. Usually, this distracts the lizard's enemy long enough for the lizard to escape. But don't worry, this does not harm the lizard. In just a few short weeks, it will grow a brand new, shorter tail.

"True" Lizards

When most people think of lizards, they probably picture one with four legs and a tail that is usually longer than its body. This is the classic description of the family *Lacertidae,* also sometimes called "true" lizards. They were probably given this name because they were some of the first to be studied by scientists.

Lacertids are small- to medium-sized creatures and many are brilliantly colored. They eat insects, spiders, scorpions, and small vertebrates. This type of lizard is found in Europe, Asia, and Africa, and some live as far north as the Arctic Circle.

This lacertid is known as the Green Lizard. It's easy to see why!

*Most geckos are brown or gray and active
mainly at night. But this Mauritius Day Gecko
is brightly colored and prefers to be up and
around in the daytime.*

Houseguests

While most lizards try to stay as far away from people as possible, geckos often move right in with them. In hot countries where they thrive, "house geckos" may even live like pets in people's homes. They earn their keep by eating insects. Thanks to special pads on the bottom of their feet they can walk straight up walls or across ceilings, just like a fly. And they have retractable claws for rough surfaces, such as trees.

Most geckos are 2 to 6 inches (5 to 15 centimeters) long. Their skin is almost transparent and only a few have moveable eyelids. The others have clear scales called spectacles that cover and protect their eyes.

Geckos are the most vocal of all the lizards. The sounds they make range from the hoarse "geh-ho" that gives them their name to soft chirps and loud shrieks.

Quick Change Artists

True chameleons live in Africa and Asia and are famous for their ability to change color. Although they may blend in with their surroundings, this is not the reason for the color change. They are simply reacting to changes in temperature, light conditions, or even moods.

Most chameleons live in trees and can grip branches with their toes and tail. They can also look in two directions at the same time, and many have horns or spines on their head. Unlike many lizards, however, chameleons cannot grow a new tail if they lose the one they have.

Chameleons eat insects, but they move so slowly it's a wonder they ever catch anything. If it weren't for their amazing tongue, they probably wouldn't. Remaining perfectly still, the chameleon waits for an insect to come within striking range. In a flash it shoots out its tongue—which is at least as long as its body—and captures the insect with the sticky tip. It reels in the catch and dinner is served.

Zap!

Slinky Skinks

The largest family of lizards in the world is the skink family. There are over 1,200 different species of skinks, and they are found on every continent except Antarctica. Most make their home in climates that are warm year-round, but a few live in southern Canada where winters are cold. These species hibernate all winter.

Skinks are sleek creatures with rounded bodies. Most are quite small and have four small legs and a tail that is longer than their body. Burrowing skinks have tiny legs or no legs at all, however, and they have a clear window in their lower eyelid so that they can see underground when their eyes are closed! Some skinks eat only plants, while others eat insects, spiders, worms, and even small mice.

Although they are quite active, skinks are secretive creatures and so, they are rarely seen. If you want to see one for yourself, try looking under rocks, in moist decaying logs, or under leaves. If you do find one, you'd better not grab it Not only will it drop its tail—it may bite.

Opposite page:

While most skinks are slim and have long tails, the Stump-tailed Skink is an exception. As its name suggests, it has a short, stumpy tail, which looks a lot like its head. Can you tell which end of these skinks is which?

Mighty Monitors

Meet the giants of the lizard world, the monitors. Although most are not much more than a foot (30 centimeters) long, some of these beasts can grow to a length of 10 feet (3 meters)!

The largest monitor, the Komodo Dragon, has been known to eat a sheep for dinner, and all of them will eat just about anything they can catch. A special lower jaw, which can unhinge from the skull and swing down, enables them to swallow much of their prey whole and the largest in a few big chunks.

There are about 30 species of monitor lizard, all of them living in the tropics. They can be found in fields or jungles, and many spend a lot of time in trees. Most monitors are good swimmers.

A Komodo Dragon may weigh up to 300 pounds (135 kilograms)!

Whiptail.

Fleet of Foot

When it comes to speed not many reptiles can match the members of the *Teiidae* family. With their long, slender bodies, straight legs, and extra-long tails, these lizards are built for speed. Some species can reach up to 18 miles (29 kilometers) per hour. That's an incredible 27 feet (8 meters) a second. Bet you can't move that fast!

These active lizards range in size from 4 to 48 inches (10 to 120 centimeters), but most come about halfway in between. Because of their quickness and long skinny tail, some are known as Racerunners and Whiptails. The scales on their upper body are small and rounded and don't overlap. This allows them to move easily and gives them a velvety appearance.

Most Whiptails eat insects, worms, and snails, although larger teiids eat small mammals, birds, eggs, and other reptiles. In all, there are more than 200 members of this family. Most are found in South America, with a few in the United States.

Iguanas, Big and Little

The *Iguanidae* are a large family of lizards of almost 700 species. Most are found in North and South America. The smallest ones are a mere 4 inches (10 centimeters) in length, and the largest are 6 feet (2 meters) long. While most eat plants and fruit, others, especially young iguanas, eat insects and other small invertebrates.

The most impressive member of this family is the Common Iguana, the largest lizard found in the Americas. It looks like a dinosaur with a fringe of scales running down its back to the base of its tail. Like most iguanas, it has a *dewlap*. or loose flap of skin, under its throat. This dewlap can be puffed out when the lizard wants to challenge another lizard or impress its mate.

With its sharp claws, the Common Iguana is an excellent climber and can scamper up trees like a squirrel. Despite its size, it is very quick and can outrun a dog on the ground. Not bad for a lizard!

Deep-Sea Divers

You might not expect to find lizards in the ocean, but that is where Marine Iguanas spend a lot of their time. They live on the rocky beaches of the Galapagos Islands in the Pacific Ocean.

A Marine Iguana is perfectly suited for its life in and around the water. It has a long, flat tail that it uses to push itself through the water and long curved claws that help it climb out onto the rocks.

Marine Iguanas feed on seaweed and algae. Although they prefer to eat along the shoreline, at times they must dive as deep as 50 feet (16 meters) to find food. These incredible divers can stay underwater for almost an hour before surfacing for air. They live in large groups called *colonies*. In a typical colony, the rocks are covered with wall-to-wall lizards.

No, it isn't a dinosaur—it's a Marine Iguana.

Worm Lizards and Horned Toads

Although most lizards live on the ground or in trees, some types actually spend their whole life underground. People often mistake these burrowing lizards for worms. For this reason, they are known as Worm Lizards. Their bodies have adapted to life below ground—most have no legs, which makes it easier for them to move through soil. Their eyes are very small because they are rarely used, and many worm lizards have pale skin. They may be up to 16 inches (40 centimeters) long, and they feed on small insects.

The Horned Lizard is another very unusual type. Although it is also called a horned toad, it is not a toad, but a lizard with a short tail. The Horned Lizard is 3 to 7 inches (7.5 to 18 centimeters) long and has a flat body with sharp spikes on its head and back to protect it from enemies. But that isn't its only method of self-defense. Some Horned Lizards can also squirt blood from their lower eyelids! Many animals, such as wild dogs, lose their appetite for lizard after such a display.

Horned Lizard.

Leaping Lizards

You know that lizards can swim, run, burrow, and climb trees, but did you know that one species can glide through the air? Known as the Draco, or flying dragon, it is a member of the *Agamidae* family and lives in Asia and Indonesia.

The Draco has long flexible ribs that can be spread out from its body like an umbrella, revealing a large pair of skin flaps. Leaping from a branch high in a tree, it glides through the air like a paper airplane. When at rest, the Draco is rather dull-colored and looks more like an insect than a lizard.

It's a bird . . . it's a plane . . . it's a flying Draco!

Handle with Care

The *Anguidae* are a very old family of lizards. They either have tiny legs and toes, or no legs or feet at all. Tough scales form rings around their body like a coat of armor.

One of the most interesting anguids is the Glass Lizard. Also known as the Glass Snake, this bizarre creature looks like a snake and has shiny, smooth scales. It gets its name from the fact that its fragile tail will break off if handled roughly. Its flickering tongue makes it appear even more snakelike. Glass Snakes range from 2 to 3 feet (60 to 90 centimeters) in length, and they eat insects, small mammals, and other lizards.

Would you recognize this Glass Snake as a lizard? Well, that's what it is.

It's best to keep your distance from the Gila Monster.

Lethal Lizards

While most lizards are harmless, there are two species you wouldn't want to mess around with. They are the Gila (pronounced *hee-luh*) Monster and the Mexican Beaded Lizard, and they're the only poisonous lizards in the world. Both species live in the desert and are quite colorful. They are mainly *nocturnal,* sleeping most of the day away in a moist, dark burrow.

The 2-foot (60-centimeter)-long Gila and its slightly larger Mexican cousin have cheeks that appear to be swollen. This is where their *venom glands* are located. Unlike snakes, these lizards do not have long fangs for injecting poison into their victims. Instead, they have special grooved teeth. When they bite, they hang on for as long as possible while the venom flows from their mouth into the wound. Although the poison can kill small animals, it is rarely fatal to people.

Helping Out

Now that you know more about lizards, you would probably like to meet one face-to-face some day. And if you are alert enough and lucky enough to do so, you are likely to enjoy the experience because lizards are not only fascinating but can also be quite beautiful.

However, if you are still a little nervous about their scaly skin, unusual habits, and sharp claws, remember that almost any lizard will be at least as nervous about you. It's also important to remember that lizards are very useful. They eat millions of insects and other small pests that may ruin crops or be harmful to other animals and to people.

In some countries, lizards are even thought to bring good luck. So much so, in fact, that in parts of Southeast Asia people are reluctant to move into a new house until a Tokay, a type of gecko, has moved in. What a strange and wonderful houseguest to have!

Words To Know

Amphibians   A group of animals that live both on land and in water. Frogs, toads, and salamanders are amphibians.

Cold-blooded   The term used to describe animals that have no automatic internal control of their body temperature.

Colony   A group of the same kind of animals living together.

Dewlap   A flap of loose skin that hangs from the neck of some animals.

Gland   A part of an animal's body that makes and gives out substances.

Hibernate   To fall into a kind of heavy sleep during the winter. When animals hibernate, their breathing and heart rates slow, and their body temperatures go down.

Invertebrate   An animal without a backbone.

Keratin   The protein that forms the basis of horns, nails, hair, feathers, and scales.

Mate   To come together to produce young. Either member of an animal pair is also the other's mate.

Mating season   The time of year when animals come together to produce young.

Nocturnal   The term used to describe animals that are active at night.

Prey   An animal that other animals hunt for food.

Reptile   A class of cold-blooded animals that includes snakes, alligators, turtles, and lizards.

Salamander   An amphibian with a tail that has moist, scaleless skin and breathes through gills in the larva stage.

Scale   The thin, hard overlapping plate that protects a lizard's skin.

Species   A class or kind of animal that has certain traits in common.

Venom   A poisonous fluid produced by some lizards.

Index

PHOTO CREDITS
Cover: Bill Ivy. **Interiors:** Boyd Norton, 4, 31; Bill Ivy, 7, 8a, 8b, 11, 12, 28, 39, 44; Doug Wechsler (Vireo), 15; K. H. Switak (Photo Researchers) 16; Zoological Society of San Diego, 18-19, 35, 42; Stock Market Inc., 20; Fco. Márquez, 23; Tom McHugh (Photo Researchers), 24, 41; Stephen Dalton (Photo Researchers), 27; Ron Garrison (Zoological Society of San Diego), 32; Ron Dengler (Network), 36.